Single Motherhood: The Real Deal

D.C. Spencer

authorHOUSE®

AuthorHouse™
1663 Liberty Drive
Bloomington, IN 47403
www.authorhouse.com
Phone: 1-800-839-8640

First published by AuthorHouse   9/1/2009

ISBN: 978-1-4490-2413-0 (e)
ISBN: 978-1-4490-2411-6 (sc)
ISBN: 978-1-4490-2412-3 (hc)

Library of Congress Control Number: 2009909039

Printed in the United States of America
Bloomington, Indiana

This book is printed on acid-free paper.

Dedication

To God, blessing me with the knowledge and the will to write this book. And to my daughter my joy and my heart, without her this wouldn't have been possible. To everyone else who believed in me and encouraged me to give life to my ideas by putting them on paper.

Acknowledgments

My book cover was possible by Ron Brooks, who took the time to help bring forth my idea. Traci Hearn and Katrina Carmichael and everyone else for listening to my ideas and making sure I stayed in the right direction, when my thoughts got the best of me, and everyone who helped me out at long the way. Lastly, the two women who had a great influence in my life, my mother and grandmother, they showed me what it takes to be a mother. *Love, Patience, Good Listener, and Time*

Peace of Mind

I wrote this book for two reasons. The first is so that my child could understand who I am as a single mother. I hope it will allow her to look past the image she has of me as a mother and see the woman who chose to have her. The second reason I wrote this book is for myself as a form of self-therapy to cleanse my soul, my spirit, and my mind of the guilty feelings of not being the mother I truly wanted to be for my child.

So, as you read and ponder my words, know that they are from the heart. These are the personal experiences of not just one mother, but many single mothers. Being a single mother is not a club, but a rite of passage. An experience of one's self, where you will lose, find, and restructure yourself, all for the love of a child.

Induction

In today's society the definition of motherhood is to create, give birth, care for, and protect. Well that's society's meaning. The real-world meaning of motherhood is to provide by any means necessary, like a lioness protecting her cub. Protecting that child from the time they are conceived, throughout birth, and thereafter. We will provide for our child at any cost. Motherhood might break down every fiber of your being and push your back to the wall. There will be moments when you might lose yourself and forget who you are—all that is from caring for that child at any cost.

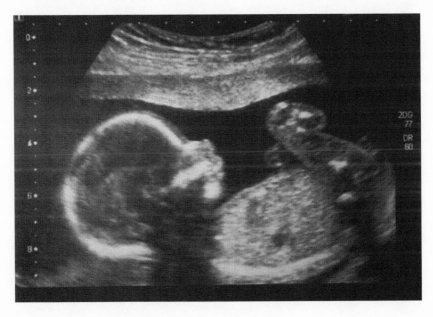

Choices

So you believe you're pregnant and need to inform your man that he's the father. First things first, please make sure you are pregnant. Count the day from your last period to now, that's the only way to know for sure. Take yourself to the nearest drugstore and purchase a pregnancy test. Rush back home, gather the phone, and dash for the bathroom to confirm if your feelings are true.

Rip open the package, pop your butt on the toilet, and hold the stick between your spread legs, releasing the floodgates of your bladder. Soak the stick completely in urine, and replace it back on the discarded box. Nervously wait for the magical symbol to appear, which holds the faith of your uncertainty in its hands.

When the answer comes out yes, you can do one of two things. One, you curse yourself, or two, thank the Lord for your blessing. But either way, takes a deep breath and exhales; that part is over. Or is it? Because in a brief moment the hard reality of motherhood will hit home, throwing your world into a never-ending black hole. You question your very judgment, doubting yourself. Should you even tell him or keep the baby? Honey, when these thoughts start to cloud your mind, there are three letters that will release you from this pain. Three letters you should never forget, **TAK.** What, you've never heard of **TAK?** Allow yourself to be enlightened: Terminated, Adoption, or Keep it?

Yes, it's a hard choice to make, but it has to be done. For that percent of women who decide to keep the baby, letting the father know is the next hurdle. Even here you have a choice to make. Will it be over the phone or in person? No matter what you choose to do or say, the words will still be the same.

"Guess what? I'm pregnant."

"Guess who's going to be a father?"

"I guess we had a little too much fun, because I am pregnant."

"You always said one day you wanted to start a family."

"The condom must have broken, because I am pregnant."

"The pill didn't work and I am pregnant."

"You're a daddy."

"I am pregnant, so what you want to do?"

After he gets over the shock of your words, prepare yourself for the emergence of his true identity. Really study his facial expression, because he could be bluffing you. Read his eyes—that's where the true emotion lies. Listen to the words coming out of his mouth, but remember the eyes hold the key to his true feelings.

"What am I supposed to do?"

"You're sure it's mine?"

"Damn, I thought that condom broke."

"Man, I knew I should have pulled out sooner."

"I will be there for you."

"I thought you took care of that so this wouldn't happen."

"How much does the clinic cost?"

"It can't be mine because I double up."

Now you have a baby daddy, someone to help you out in your time of need to give you moral support and a shoulder to cry on while assisting you financially and spiritually in the rearing of your child. Now what type of help you will receive, that's a different story. Something we will get more into later, but for now live in the bliss of your newborn family.

One + One = Baby and Me

The next obstacle, and the hardest, is informing your family. As fear engulfs your very soul, know there's no easy way. The choice is yours. What will be the easiest and the safest way? Whether it's e-mail, videotape, video e-mail, a written letter, a card, in person, or over the phone, either way it has to be done. Remember, you can't play the hiding game forever or tell everyone that you're gaining weight. Lies. Lies. Soon or later your belly will show and the cat will be out of the bag.

Come on ladies, you know we have those friends, mothers, grandmothers, and relatives who you can't hide anything from. Somehow or some way they know what your next move will be before you even put it into action. Now, you think your parents want to hear this life changing news from them or you? Let's be for real. These people open their mouths at the wrong time, for the wrong reason, and it's always during a special event or at family get together.

Look, do yourself a favor and just tell your parents. Let them kill, slice, and dice you with their words, because when the storm clouds clear, they will be waiting for you with open arms. Those are the lucky ones. Sadly, there are a few parents out there who will disown their children for this one mistake. In their world of disillusion they have the right to disown you by dismissing you from their lives. They will write you out of the family will for this little act of disloyalty. They will shut you out in your time of need. Maybe in time they will forgive you or they won't. Only you can take this ball of negative energy, flip it and turn it around, use it to find your inner strength. Step up and bless this child by being the best parent you can be, by showing this child the love that was denied to you.

A MOTHER'S PRAYER

As I lay you down to sleep

I pray that I am the mother you will keep

My love I will give

My heart you will take

For the life we will share

On the journey we will take

As the Lord bless us each day

For now I lay you down to sleep

Amen

Birth and Responsibility

Well, your time is near, and you're due any time or any minute. No matter what book you read or what anyone says, this is a painful, risky, wonderful, and scary experience. Do you have your bag packed? One thing is for sure; it's nothing like the movies. You'll never know when it's going to happen, when that life within you pushes its way out, it will sneak up on you. For nine months, you were one body, one soul, and two heartbeats walking on this earth. The world you once knew is changing.

There you are, lying in the hospital bed, breathing between pains of contraction. Or you might be one of the fortunate ones who sleep through their labor pains. (I did.) Hard to believe, it's true and rare. However intense the pain maybe, you'll survey the occupants of the room, as everyone waits breathlessly for your bundle of joy to be delivered. For you it's not the delivery, but hoping your baby daddy will show up on time or just be there to share this wonderful moment. Make sure you have someone to take pictures. This will be your way to remember the moment and remember who was there and who wasn't there.

All the hoping and finger crossing won't make your baby daddy show up. It's up to them to be man enough to show up. Remember, it's their choice. If you have your baby daddy by your side, asks yourself, is he there because he wants to be or is it a front? If you didn't know, you will know now. There's a difference. Now the front man will say all the right things, his manner is sweet, caring, and everything an expectant father should be. You must ask yourself, why is he so attentive now. When you had important doctors and ultrasound appointments and needed a ride, where was he? Nowhere to be found. His actions make you wonder about his hidden agenda. I applaud the twenty-five percent or less of men who are there because they want to be. I applaud them for stepping up to the mike and being a real man, because they understand their responsibility and know that it took more than one person to make a baby. They know that things cost and they will be your rock and your co-partner raising that child. Thank the Lord for blessing you with this man, who will be by your side every day.

The birth of your child is a beautiful thing. But sorry to say, there is a dark side that no one talks about—mothers who hide their pregnancy for nine months and then trash their unwanted child. Sad to say, these are single mothers who can't handle motherhood. The very thought of motherhood, that great change, scares them. They wonder what would people would say and think. They are embarrassed to tell their family. The pain is so great and the only way they see to release this pain is to get rid of the cause of the pain. If your pregnancy comes to this point, and you're drowning in guilt and shame, please, do not trash or harm your baby. There are many safe havens where you can take your child. As stated before this is a touchy subject, but a lot of single mothers out there are blind to the fact that there is a law out there called "The Infant Safe Haven Law."

This law is set up to help mothers who feel they are in a crisis to safely relinquish their baby at a haven where the child will be protected and provided with medical care until a permanent home can be found.

As of February 2008, almost all fifty states have set up some type of Safe Haven provision for unwanted babies by parents who can't handle parenthood. The law is set up to allow the parent, a friend of the parent, or another family member to safely surrender the infant at a safe haven. These safe havens are police or fire departments, a hospital emergency room, a licensed physician, a nurse or other licensed healthcare worker, an EMS provider, an adoption agency, a responsible adult, or the child welfare department. By choosing to do it this way, you save yourself from being prosecuted for abandonment, neglect, or murder. The child must be alive when you drop them off. Yes, you can be anonymous; they are more worried about the child than you. Welcome to the privileged world of anonymity and immunity; all this can be forfeited and charges brought against you if there are signs of abuse or neglect.

Follow these simple guidelines if you are planning to deliver your child to a safe haven:

1. Leave written information on the family medical history of the child when you relinquish your child.
2. When you relinquish your child, the baby should be in an unharmed condition, with no signs of malnutrition, burns, bruises, internal and external bleeding, poisoning, bone fractures, mental distress, extreme pain, and death.
3. The child shouldn't have been abused sexually. Sexual abuse includes rape, sodomy, molestation, sexual fondling, or incest.

4. There should not be any signs of diminished psychological capacity in the child. In other words, the child should be able to function as any other normal child of their age.

When you relinquish your baby, most states will transfer the child to the department that handles child protective or child welfare cases. The department is responsible for placing the child in a pre-adoptive home, while petitioning the court for termination of the birth parent's parental rights. Some states have procedures in place where the parent can reclaim their child within a specified time period before any petition to terminate is granted. You may want to give up your rights to the child. In some states the birth father has the right to petition for custody of that child.

So far there are sixteen states that have set up provisions for parents to reclaiming their child. These states are: California, Connecticut, Delaware, Florida, Idaho, Illinois, Iowa, Kentucky, Louisiana, Michigan, Missouri, Montana, New Mexico, Rhode Island, and Tennessee. Out of the fifty states, Washington, DC legislation has not addressed the issue of safe haven laws. However, parents in DC can relinquish their child to the Child and Family Services office only after the child is seventy-two hours old.

As of July 2007, the "Child Welfare Information Gateway" has set up information regarding each state's safe haven law on their Web site (www.childwelfare.gov). Another Web site to help you understand the states' laws regarding safe havens is the National Safe Haven Alliance (www.nationalsafehavenalliance. org). Their phone is 1-888-510-Baby. These are just two of many Web sites out there that can help you. *Remember that laws do change, so check your state to see where they stand on safe havens for infants.* It's better to be safe than sorry. Still unsure? Take some parenting classes and some books on how to be a parent.

For those who embrace the ordeal of giving birth and keeping your child, enjoy the little blessing that you helped create and bring forth into this world. This child will always be a part of you, no matter what you do. So, love and rejoice in your blessing that was bestowed upon you.

Responsibility. What's the meaning? Do you know? Society states it's a thing or person that one is responsible for. When it comes to your child, responsibility means loyalty, obligation, being dependable, reliable, and stable. But it is most important that your child feels they can trust you and have faith in you.

Along with responsibility comes sacrifice. Some of you don't believe that sacrifice has to be made. Yet you already made one by choosing to have your baby. That's the biggest sacrifice of all, your choice to keep your baby. You may not see it or understand it, but down the road you will.

Going home, leaving the hospital and the nurses waiting on you behind, reality closes in. The responsibility of your child is in your hands now. It's your job to care, provide, and comfort your little one. You have to ask yourself can you handle it. Because the things you used to do, like partying, drinking, shopping till you drop, getting high, and leaving on Friday and coming back on Monday (or the following Friday), all this must stop. You have to be woman enough to put those things to the side and put your child first.

Some of you haven't accepted the fact that this child needs you more than you need yourself. So stop being scared and get off your behind and take care of your child. When that child is crying during the night, needing to be held, fed, and changed, who's going to do it? Not your mother or baby daddy, no one but you. Ever heard, "You had it, you take care of it"? They were not talking about baking a cake or changing the oil in your car. Can you handle that responsibility when it comes knocking at the door?

Please stop with the notion that your mom, aunts and uncles, grandma, godparents, or whoever will watch the child. They didn't give birth to the child. Where do you get off, disposing your child your child at so-an-so's house and coming back after days on end? I know what you're thinking. I take the child over to my mom's house for a visit. A visit is one to six hours, while anything over twenty-four hours is a sign of abandonment. We all know the reason why you do; the walls are closing in around you, with you barely keeping your head above water. You are looking for some much-needed adult conversation.

You put your child's life in jeopardy every time you walk out the door. Ask yourself—is it worth it? Remember there are pedophiles in all walks of life. A pedophile is an older adult or adolescent who's sexually attracted to children under the age of consent. And most states the age of consent is sixteen. Check out Ms. or Mr. So-and-So before you leave your child with them. It's better to be safe than sorry.

With responsibility come choices. And there are some hard decisions to be made, from choosing a new outfit, a pair of glasses, or buying that latest CD or DVD, to purchasing clothes, diapers, and formula for the baby. Everything you want or need for yourself will take a back seat to that child. From taking your birthday or Christmas money to pay bills, to returning items you purchased for yourself, to taking jobs that are beneath you, every move you make must be in the child's best interest.

Responsibility is a mixing pot of many different things from loyalty to obligation. You will feel moral ties to your child, and a sense of duty. You must build a foundation made of trust and support. You will be strong and devoted to each other. You will offer stability in a world of uncertainty.

You will lose yourself to the point where you question your own actions Responsibility is hard in this world for the single mothers; you have no one to turn to but yourself. Don't be scared. There are a few people who will support you and stand by your side with open and helping arms.

Your child is a gift to you from God. How you raise that child is your gift to God.

The System

The system will not discriminate against any individual or group because of race, sex, religion, age, national origin, color, height, weight, marital status, political beliefs, or disability. But it will break your spirit and belittle you to the point of no return. It doesn't matter if you're a well-educated, independent, take the bull by the horns type of woman. The system is made to break you and it will.

The system is another form of government slavery. How could this be in the land of milk and honey? Well, it's been going on for many years. We just call it the welfare system, or FIP (Family Independence Program). It's a program where you receive health insurance, food stamps, and cash allowances. Basically, it's a poverty stricken program for the poor and the unemployed.

There are two different types of women in the system. One we already know, because everyone has at least one in his or her family. These are the ones who go back to when the system started with Franklin Roosevelt, during the Depression. Or as

15

we call them, the welfare generation. Grandmothers, mothers, and daughters, all on the system living by the motto: "the more babies I have, the system will gladly take care of them." They know all the ins and outs; to the point you believe they must have a secret handbook of their very own. Because these women always get what they want, working the system to the best of their ability. Now the other half, they are the ones with their backs to the wall and nowhere to turn. The women out there who are unemployed, with one or two children, who lost their jobs or maybe going to school, just happened to get pregnant. We are the ones who are down on our luck and new to the system, and we're the ones the system chews up and spits out. The price we must pay, for a little help to restart our lives. Please believe this is not a life choice, but a temporary stop on the journey of getting your life back on track.

You walk through the doors and up to the counter to receive your booklet. Yes, the booklet where you sign your identity away to become nothing but a number. Digits, notation, tattoo to your very soul. That's how they recognize you, by that evil number. V123456789. The waiting room or the holding pen is where you sit till someone comes from behind the black or sliver steel door to call your name. With unsure steps, you venture down the short hallway to the waiting table, where the person (your caseworker) sits across from you, mentally drilling you about the booklet you just filled out. It makes you wonder how you even got dressed that morning. But remember in their little world, they are doing you a favor by taking the time out in their busy day to help you out.

Sitting there, feeling like some mindless idiot, while your caseworker asks you to see a doctor, because their mind is swimming with skepticism. They think you're too brainless to know if you're pregnant or not. "Oh my goodness that's gas growing my stomach, when I took the test it said it was a baby." It's their job to talk you into seeing one of their clinic doctors, even when you feel safe with your own obstetrician. Just because the state is footing the bill, the questions at hand are, are you willing to take that chance with your baby? That's the choice you must make and live with.

The FIP will tell you a lot of ways how they will help you, but you must ask yourself, who's going to pay for this? They know you can't pay, if you did you wouldn't be there. To get their money back, they need to know who your baby's father is. They will ask for his name, address, and social security number, and maybe his last place of employment. All of this will help them get the ball rolling so he can help pay child support and for them to get their money back. This will get you into the Friend of the Court System, another form of government slavery. He pays into the system, FIP gets their cut, and you get what's left over. If you had any plans of not letting anyone know who the baby's natural father is, you better come up with something, because FIP won't even help you unless you tell them what the baby's father name is.

Bring your driver's license or state ID, and you and your child's social security card. Do not forget rent receipts, and utility bills, like phone, light, water, and heat. Sorry, no cell phone bills (that's a luxury). The most important thing is that you must verify your income by letting them know if you have a job and a checking and savings account. Any money coming in they want to know about, because that will determine on how much you will receive in food stamps and cash allowance, or as they call it now your bridge card. Everything is placed on this card. Oh, there's one more thing. They feel they must know how many people are living in your home and how to get to your house. Just in case they feel the need to stop by. Some workers will, and that's what happened to a friend of mine. Her worker decided to pop over to her house. The worker told her, "Why do you need aid, when your house is so nice?" The worker failed to see that this wasn't her house, but her parent's house, which were nice enough to let her live there. But if that worker looked at her records, they would have known she was at the age where her parents were no longer providing for her. She was welcome to stay there, but anything else was on her. Another single mother, who was eight and half months pregnant, lost her job. Her caseworker wanted her to go to Work First and a find a job. But luckily, Work First couldn't help her till after the baby was born. So she had take a parenting class for misguided mothers. She had to take the classes or she wouldn't receive her money or food allowance. But it was okay for the caseworker to take two months after the baby was born turn on the child's insurance. The worker just chalked that up to the fact that they didn't have time because they had a heavy caseload.

Here's another great way the system works. A lady wanted childcare for her child, which the system will pay for. It just took her six months to receive her childcare money, by that time she already had a job and they wanted to review her case for money she didn't receive. Your caseworker won't help you unless they feel you are down on your luck without a pot to piss in. Then in their eyes they feel you are needy and should be glad to receive any help they are willing to give you. We are willing to take any table scraps that the master is willing to throw our way, for the simple reason that the master always wants his slaves to be grateful that he is taking care of them.

Oh, if this is not enough, wait till you attend Work First, or, as they call it now, WF/JET (Work First/Jobs, Education and Training). This little program is set up to help you get back into the workforce. When can't find a job or don't have a job, this is they send you. Sometimes you'll be the most educated person sitting up there. There are a few people who never graduated from high school, who are lacking the skills needed for filling out an application or going out on a job interview. The JET program is set up to train these people how to find a job and get out the welfare system's pocket.

Don't even thing about not going to JET. That's a no-no, because if you don't they'll have the right to deny your case. Isn't that sweet? There are three major problems with this program. The first is that they hire workers who don't know what they are doing. These people are there just for a paycheck and don't care about you. Half the time you're older than the person working there. Second, they need to separate the people who know from the people who don't know. Why on earth would you put someone who has college or high school degree and work experience in the same class with someone who doesn't? If that person has a degree, you should you help them find a job in that field, instead of trying to find them a job flipping burgers or working at some job for pennies. Lastly, the major problem with the JET program is this. If you're in the system and trying to go to college or a trade school, well you might as well forget it. In your eyes, you're trying to better yourself to get off the system. They see it as a waste of time and you should be there looking for a job, instead going to school and sitting around waiting to collect your check, even when you know that when you finish with school you will have a job.

Think I am joking? I am not. They will send you letters in the mail saying that if you don't report to FIP by a particular date you will be cut off. I know people who are in school who had the teacher or counselor call FIP to explain their dilemma. All to be told by their caseworker and the workers of at FIP that they should quit school and if they want to keep their case open. They feel that you are cheating the system for wanting a better life.

It all goes back to the fact that master doesn't want to see his slaves leave the plantation. For the simple reason that they might find something out there that is a little better than what they all ready have. Because when you teach someone to fend for her and herself, they don't need you anymore. And you lose what little control you have on them. So break the chains and free yourself by going to some type of school and get the training you need to break away from "hold them back by any means necessary slave holders."

You have to remember that the welfare system sees us as preschool material when we walk through their doors. We are little children that must be led by the hand, who failed at our freedom and responsibility of life, and whose every move must be watched. The system can help and destroy your self-esteem all in one single blow. So watch your back and your soul when you enter those lustrous doors. Please try not to forget who you are and remember this is only a temporary stop to a better life. One more thing, pray that you get a caseworker who cares and sees you more as person than a number, or a person who has their hand out trying to get something for free. Just because you signed that dotted line, remember it's for help, not a way to sign your soul away.

Here a few little things I found out myself. If you want an increase in your child support payment and you are in the system, the best thing to do is wait till you are completely off and out of the system. (Just remember once in the system always in the system.) When you get that job you want, wait until you get your ninety days in and have been there for a couple of months and your health insurance kicks in. At this time you need to take yourself down to the friend of the court and start filling out the much-needed forms for an increase in your child support. Since now you have a "real" job that can pay the bills, the state/system will no longer take your child support money, but instead the money comes to you. You can ask for an increase every two years and get your daycare paid for and maybe some of your medical bills. For it to really work get off the system and break the chains.

There's another system out there that has an effect on the single mother. It doesn't pertain to the adult single mother; it has more of bearing on the teenage single mother. You know, the people we like to dust under the rug so we don't have to think about them or look at them. Out of sight, out of mind, that's what the school system believes.

It started back in the mid 60s when the board of education set up schools that would deal with the growing problem of infant mortality and premature births among teen mothers. The main reason for these schools was to educate these girls who were damaged by negative life experiences. The schools were designed to show them a totally new and positive life experience by helping them cope with motherhood by improving their self-esteem and their performance in school.

That's the old way of doing things, but in today's world things are very different. These schools are nothing but a dumping ground and a wasteland for pregnant girls. It's where the schools system brushes you off to when you start to show. I guess they feel that you are an embarrassment to the school or that by being pregnant you can't fit into the school's way of doing things. It's understandable for insurance reasons that the school doesn't want to be responsible for the child welfare if something goes wrong, for the simple reason they will be setting themselves up for a lawsuit. Lawsuit or not, they shouldn't be dumping these girls into the vast wasteland of nothingness that will never help them out in the long run.

As a parent, you need to ask yourself—why you are letting the school system do this to your daughter. Throughout history, women fought too hard to be treated as an equal when it comes to education to be thrown into a wasteland because of one night of indiscretion. That's right, a wasteland, something that few people knows about. Basically when it comes down to it, all depends on the school distract you live in. Sorry to say, the better the district, the better the care you will receive.

In the school system, the job of security is to watch over our children to make sure they stay out of harm's way. When did it become their job to watch to see if your daughter looks pregnant? If she looks like she's putting on weight or is looking a little too fat, they have the right to take your child to the principal's office and question her. They can make her take a pregnancy test, and if she's found out to be pregnant, she must leave the school right away. Or, better yet, if she has a miscarriage and wants to return to school, the school might refuse because they still believe that child is pregnant. In both cases, the child would have to sit out of school. What gives them that right, or did we give them right to treat our daughters any way they choose?

The problem is that the schools that these girls are attending are not helping them, but basically holding them back. What are they teaching them? Nothing that is beneficial. When you come back to school, you're a year or two behind your friends. You have received an "F" for the classes you missed. You're sitting there not taking any classes that you need to help prepare yourself for returning back into the mainstream of life. The school system is saying it isn't their fault that you got yourself knocked up, had to drop out, and are now behind in school.

The school system should set up a system where the schools can work as one system to help each other out by offering parenting classes and in-school daycare. By having a daycare place in the school, this would cut down the dates the girl would have to miss because there's no sitter to be found. The parenting classes would help them face and understand their responsibilities and give them the courage they need to take charge of their life and raise a family. It's already hard out there for a single mother, why does the school system have to make it even harder?

Baby Daddies

Here's the much waited for chapter, explaining the different classifications of baby daddies. You may be surprised what you read. After the birth of your child, know that your sperm donor's (your baby's father) true identity will emerge. His actions will speak louder than his words. Words can be nothing but deception. Their actions will enlighten you to their inner truth. Let the revelation begin.

Knight in shining armor: This category has two different chivalrous groups.

1. *King Arthur.* Most in this category are older men who feel it's their job to protect you to the point of smothering you. In their mind you're a child with childlike behavior, crying out to be saved. They are trying to be heroic when all their actions fall into the father figure syndrome, by providing all the basic needs for you and your child. He will give you money when needed, but don't be surprised if he questions you for your reason for

wanting the money. He has to make sure you're not spending his money on unwanted items. Now he might even marry you or you might cohabit together. Daddy has to keep you safe. He might even sign the birth certificate.

2. *The Nobleman.* Everyone wants this man, but only a few are lucky enough to have one. He's caring, respectful, trustworthy, loving, and hard working. He understands what his responsibility is, which is being a father and a provider for your child. He's the type of man you marry and he's a good role model for your child. He wants to be a part of his child's life and your life. It's a form of dishonor for him to not sign the birth certificate and he takes care of you.

Deadbeat Daddies: This type falls into four different categories. No matter how you categorize them, they are all the same. These men have little time, little care, little love, and little respect for their child. To them a child is like a jail sentence with no parole.

1. *Street Life Daddy.* He will teach your child all the ins and outs of the streets. He'll give them an education that they will never forget. You hope they don't get your child caught up in their hot, troubled mess. Oh, child support, good question—not unless he has a front job. With this type of man, it's sometimes best to get an insurance policy on them, for the simple reason that you can't pay child support with an illegal job. You hope and pray that this man lives long enough to see his child come of age. Make sure they sign the birth certificate, because you have to remember a street life daddy will end up one of four ways: surviving, handicapped, in prison, or dead.

2. *Prison Daddies.* These are men behind bars trying to be a father while doing three years or more or even life. Prison daddies are trying to hold onto what they can't have, their little piece of reality they have left. They hope their children and their women will carry them though. If that child is born before or during their jail time they are proud fathers who can't accept the fact that you might move on without them. They may want to see their child, but they have to understand and accept the fact that maybe that child doesn't want to see them. In their eyes, how can a man they don't know be their dad? Here they are behind bars, playing daddy and barking orders to an empty chair, an empty space in their life. Now on the other side of things, there are a few women and children who stand by their prison daddy. Because they know who this man was and still is before he went behind bars. Bring the children in for their weekly and monthly visits with their father. Let them know that even bars can't hold them back from being their father. You have to understand it's hard for these men to show you their love, or provide for you, behind bars. A jail cell can't get the bills paid or buy milk and diapers.

3. *Mind Game Daddies.* These are the great intimidators. These men will use your emotions against you. They will have you doubting yourself with their quick wit. For all the wrong they do, its funny how they can make it seem like it's your own fault that the child doesn't get what they need. Not showing up when you want them to, but showing up when it's convenient for them. It's your fault that he doesn't sign the birth certificate. The king of the mind games, making you mistrust your child's upbringing, to the point you feel that he can do a better job. He will walk into your life and turn it inside and out. He'll have you on your knees crying and second-guessing yourself,

telling you if you act right this wouldn't be happening. And you wouldn't have brought this on yourself. While the whole time he's walking around, so proud of himself for the chaos he caused. They are good, dangerous, and very manipulate. Manipulation, how sweet it is.

4. *Don't Give Damn Daddies.* We know them and see them on television. Men who refuse to pay child support. They have money, but don't feel the need to pay. They don't have to be superstar; they can be hamburger flipper, gas attendant, lawyer, doctor, or the average guy on the street. Their child is no thing to them, but a mistake that was made in the heat of the moment. Why should they pay for something they didn't ask for or choose to make? Why should they change their lifestyle for this unwanted child? Their motto is "You want it, you take care of it." Some pay child support, but the neglect their child in different ways. They figure we get their money, what more do we want? They don't think or see that maybe the child wants them more than money. They feel it's your attitude keeping them away. If you were a good little girl and kept your emotions to yourself, by not letting them know how you actually feel, they might choose to come around more. Remember this one rule when dealing with this type of men. Our attitude must be in check for them to be a real daddy who wants to spend real time with their child. What a caveman dream world they are living in.

Now don't get me wrong, you do have men out there who know what it means to be a true baby daddy. You know, handling his business and accepting his responsibility. If you have two or more separate baby daddies, please don't take the good one to court and screw him over to make up for what the others are doing wrong. Remember by doing this will only push him farther away and stop him for being the man you want him to be.

The world is filled with all type of dysfunctional baby daddies. The "I am broke, can't keep a job to pay child support, but am willing to babysit at my convenience" baby daddy. You bring the child for a visit at their parent's house and he never shows up. There's the married man with his mistress on the side, paying her hush money for her silence. Baby daddies think that two minutes (if that) of sexual gratification prepares them for fatherhood. It's a state of mind they must wholeheartedly accept. If he's not willing to accept it, you can always find a family practice lawyer and have them draw up the papers for your baby daddy to denounce his claim on the child. He will give up all rights to the child, legally and financially.

Why do we as single mothers feel committed to let our children have their father's last name, when there are no plans in the future for marriage? Why give the child their father's name when the relationship is already severed and you have no plans of going back? It just doesn't look right when you have one or twenty kids living in the same household with different last names. How can you explain this to your child or even how they can explain it to their friends? Remember, kids can be heartless with their teasing. Somewhere in the back of your mind, you feel that this is your little way of letting everyone know that this is his baby, or this is your way of getting back at him. Come on. As women, we have to be smarter than this. Why are we giving him credit for something that he didn't do? Remember, you're the one this child comes to for all of their needs. If he can't step up to marry you, why give prestige of showing everyone what he helped create? Know that by giving your child his or her father's last name, it doesn't make that man a father.

The Others

The others are our baby daddy's family, the extra baggage that comes along with having his child. Sometime they welcome us with open arms, and sometimes we don't talk about them too much because it's forbidden to say their names. So we whisper softly about them behind our children's back and we try our best to forget them. We don't think about them till after the baby is born. If we're lucky, they will embrace us the whole nine months before, during and after the birth of the child.

Now the nagging question in the back of your mind is what type of others will you be saddled with? The others fall into three groups: the Doubters, the Caring, and the Fakers.

The Doubters: These are your new relatives who are full of skepticism. As they sit there smiling in your face, while welcoming you and your child into their life, their mind is swimming with uncertainty of how that child could be possibly be related to them. They think that you plotted and coaxed their son into getting you pregnant. You're nothing but a money-grabbing

Jezebel or Delilah (if you don't know, these are women from the Bible), looking out for a way to escape your poor unfortunate life. Some relatives will accept the child, just because he says the child is his. It's the few who will cause you suspicion with their evil tongue, saying things like "I don't see any resemblance," or "She doesn't look like anyone in my family." These words from an unbeliever will form the seed of doubt to grow in the back of your mind. To the point whenever they see the child or the child's name is mentioned, it leads them to find something to verify their uncertainty.

Just know your world will be filled with people who accept you and reject you. So keep your guard up and your eyes and ears open to everything around you. The Doubters are the type who will have the nearest DNA clinic on speed dial or better yet, a DNA test kit safely tucked away in the house, waiting for the right moment to see if the child is really their grandchild.

The Caring: These are the ideal relatives. They will welcome you into their home with open and loving arms. They will cherish your baby, spoiling him rotten, buying him clothes and toys, or anything he wants under the sun. Some will want to spend every weekend with the child, giving you a much-needed rest. They will give you time to refresh yourself and maybe a weekend to hang out. But know this, no matter what happens between you and their son; they will want to know their grandchild. They are loving grandparents who attend every little event from birthday parties to school plays, to recitals and sporting events. Every time you enter their house, it's full of pictures of their grandchild, placed somewhere that everyone can see. They are always willing to give you loving advice on the upbringing of your child.

Know that everything they do is authentic because it's from the heart. Just remember while they are bestowing their love for their grandchild, they sometimes without thinking push you out of the way, to the point you forget who's the mother and who's the grandparent. Their TLC is the best, so enjoy them, but remember who's in charge of whom.

The Faker: They are a tricky little bunch. You never go by what they say, but more what they do. At first they seem interested in the child, waiting on pins and needles to see what the child looks like. They hover around like vultures for a month or two, or maybe a year or so before slowly fading away. Now don't think are completely gone, not these phonies, they will slowly ease back into your life, passing out their artificial love through your baby's father. They will bug him to bring the child around for holidays, birthdays, and family get-togethers. Events you will never be invited to attend. The rest of the year they care less about the child's well being. To them the child is nothing more than a toy for show and tell to take on and off the shelf when the time is right.

The Fakers will blindside your child with love and affection, leaving you to fix their little broken heart, when they no longer wanted to come around. In their minds, they are doing the right thing, because it all comes down to *you*. It's your fault they don't come around or call or stop sending gifts. Trust the Fakers as far as you can throw them. Always let their actions speak for themselves.

Remember that a person's actions speak louder than words. When dealing with others, remember what they do is more important than what they say. To bad it's not easy as rolling dice or picking out a card when it comes to dealing with the others. You can't choose or pick them, but go with the flow. You're the rudder in the storm, deciding how the flow will go. Lay your anchor, hold on tight, and say a prayer or two. Things will be rough at first; hopefully as time goes on things will get calm for you and your child.

Dating

Ready to take that deep plunge into the world of dating? Prepare yourself—it's a whole different world out there for the single mother. All the same rules of dating still hold true, but now you have to understand that you're a package deal and must be accepted as one. Remember, when it comes to relationships, one plus one equals three—you, him, and the kid. Surprise, surprise. Be you never thought you'll be called a package deal!

Truthfully, dating is hard for the single mother. Bad enough you're labeled as a package deal, but now you have to deal with men who see and treat you differently. Men have their secret little society, where there's a handbook for single women and one for the single mothers. Basically, you have to understand most men feel that, "Man was not made for woman, but a woman was made for a man." How dumb is that? You were put on this earth to satisfy a man? **Get real!** Some men feel that we should be grateful that we even have a man willing to talk to us, since we are a package deal, and all. Oh, let me bow down to the great male god.

Now don't get upset, because not all men are jackasses. There are a few good ones out there. Before we can get started, we need to weed out the worst, and we have to purge the anger we have towards our baby's father. If not, you might attract what you're trying to escape from. Don't believe me? Here's an example called "The Good and The Why-Oh-Why." First "The Good." Let's say there's this lady, who has five children (all by the same father, they never got married). She was blessed enough to meet and start dating a man who accepted her and her children. This man grew to love this woman and her children, to the point he married her and became a father to them, more of a father than their real father.

In the "Why-Oh-Why" example, here's a lady whose boyfriend got great pleasure out of belittling her, for the simple reason that it makes his day to see her mad and cry. To him it's nothing but a game of her emotional downfall. She left him, but the anger she felt for him stayed with her, to the point where she attracts nothing but men who are emotionally and physically abusive. Please resolve the anger you have towards your baby's father, so it can give you a clear head when dating.

When it comes to dating, men can sense that you're new meat, so they will try to pick you up any way they can with any line they can think of. To them, these lines work:

"Show me that pretty smile."
"When was the last time a real man made love to you?"
"Hey beautiful, what's your name?"
"I just love dark-skinned women because they are so sweet."
"You look too young to have kids."
"You're in college, so am I."
"What does your tattoo stand for or say?"
"You have the most kissable lips."

"Oh baby, don't look so mean."

"What's going on in heaven, because the angels must be falling from the sky."

"What time is? Won't you give me your name and number?

The most common phrases to come out of a man's mouth that can upset a single mother are:

+ Why can't you stay out all night?
+ Can I have or can you ask your family for some money?
+ Are you going to get back with your baby's father?
+ I know you're not complaining about buying me something, after I spend my money on you and your child.
+ I don't want to hear that you don't have any money.
+ Just because I stay here sometimes or all the time doesn't mean that I have to buy some food. Your kid eats more food than me.
+ Why can't I stay the night?
+ Do you have half or all the money for the motel room?
+ Don't act like you're broke, when I know you got money in the bank.
+ So how much money do you get for child support?
+ If you're getting child support money, you shouldn't be broke.
+ What do you mean you're tired?
+ What, you can't find someone to babysit? Does that mean you don't want to go out with me?
+ Is the kid really sick or are you just making that up?

- You need to be asking the baby's father for more money.
- When are you going to buy a car?
- Isn't about time you got your own place?
- How can you be tired when you don't do anything?
- Why can't I drive your car?

Now you would think that these men would take the time out to think before they open their mouth, because all they are doing is pissing us off. You can't stay out all night—your child might get sick or wake up in the middle of the night looking for you. And it would be rude and disrespectful to take advantage of your babysitter, that way.

When you tell a man you have no plans in this lifetime to get back with your baby's father, they don't understand. Can't they see you have no plans for him to climb back into your bed? Single mothers have to understand that your new man feels that your old man is a threat to the relationship he's trying to build with you. History you once shared with your baby's father will always be there in the way, never vanishing, every time he looks into your child's eyes. That's why must check him out and slowly bring him around your child. Hopefully we can stop all these uncalled for incidents of boyfriends taking rage out on children and using them like their personal punching bag. Now come on ladies, wake up, you didn't go through nine months of carrying this child and how many of hours of labor to have it all taken away by some loser who needs to grow up and find himself.

Single mothers, just because you are dating a man, it doesn't mean you need to give him free rein over of the things you worked to hard to achieve. Watch out for the ones to eager to move in with you, for two important reasons. It's cheaper to live with you than get their own place, because if they do that means they have to pay a bill and leave a paper trail. They just got kicked out of their last place. Also, remember you have to watch out for the pedophiles. When it comes to finding someone to watch your child, you have to do the same thing when you bring a man around your child. You have to be careful, because there are too many closet pedophiles out there who will smile in your face and win your heart, move themselves in, while the whole time trying their best to get their hands on your child and steal their innocence. So be careful of the type of man you bring around your child. Men may come and go, but remember you only have one irreplaceable child.

Single mothers; please don't let the man you're dating drive your car (unless you are in the car with him). Remember, it's cheaper for him to use yours than buy their own. It might sound nice that he's willing to help with a payment or two for the car. However, you are opening yourself up to a struggle of the wills over your ride. The ride you might have worked overtime to get, or even sacrificed to get, the same ride that is your ticket to freedom to take you and your child to wherever you want to go. No more depending on others to take you around or waiting for the bus. But now he's got you standing at the bus stop, calling for a cab, calling a ride, or calling to find him, while you're stuck somewhere waiting for him to pick you up. Come on ladies, you know this always happens when the weather is at its worse and you have somewhere important to be and can't be late. Don't put yourself in that position for disappointment, because if the car's tank needs gas, who's going to fill it? You are. If something goes wrong with it and the car needs any type of repairs, who's going to have to fix it? You are. If he receives a parking ticket or gets the car impounded, who's going to have to pay for it? You are. Now if he crashes or totals the car, who's going to pay for the repairs, the rental, and who will be out of a ride? You are. Please think before you hand over the keys to him.

As stated before, there are good men out there who will accept and respect you and your child. Sometimes they are just hard to find. They will find you when you least expect it. And sometimes they are right under your nose or right in your face. You just have to remember that the good ones are like a diamond in the rough, shining their way through.

There are some who feel that we are so dumb to have a man in our life that we will accept hurtful and vindictive words that come out of their mouth. We as single mothers will graciously accept the mental and physical abuse they dish out, while watching them flirt openly with other girls. They love to make you cry and break your will. They tell themselves, "That's another one I knew wasn't too tough to break." Don't let yourself become their little lap puppy, their faithful and mindless slave. "Oh yes master, whatever you want, I am just here to please you." How enthralled do they think we are?

Where do men get off asking a single mother for money, especially when we never ask them for any? Doesn't he understand the money we give them takes food out of our child's mouth? And that's one less bill that can be paid or one less needed outfit that we can buy. Filling their pockets is more important than giving you respect. That must be the reason why they want you to ask your family for money or give them some of your child support check. In their eyes, child supports check means man support check.

We as mothers must put an end to this shameless act. Money can always break up a relationship or a family. We have to ask ourselves why he wants us to put that type of strain your family, on the very people who have been there for us. They feel that we should walk up to our family and say, "Hey can I have some money, so me and my man can go out to night?" Or, "Can I have some money to buy that outfit or whatever expensive gift my man wants?" Or better yet, "Can I have some money for a motel room, since he said it's my turn to pay?" What parents or relative in their right mind would give you money for some crap line like that? Just remember every time you give him money, you're taking money away from your child. These men think we will do anything to keep them in our lives, because we are single mothers in need of a man. Not true!

On that note remember this—you're a package deal, not a doormat. You will find a man who will love, respect, and cherish you and your child. And maybe spoil you both.

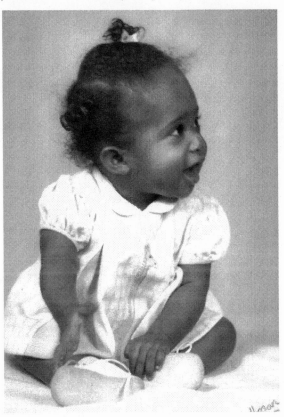

Outside World and Fix Me Sign

Maternity leave is over and it's time to return to the outside world. If you're one of the lucky ones who have a job to return to, more power to you. If not, welcome to the cruel world of the job market. Oh yes, it's vicious out there for the single mothers trying to make ends met. Everyone thinks it's easy, but really it's not. No matter how hard you plan, the rug can still be pulled out from under you.

This is how the blueprint works. First decide if you're going to work days, nights, or even weekends. Then you must think about where to work and how many hours a week, and most important what do with the baby. Remember, the child can't watch him or herself. Who will you get to babysit? A relative, your friends and neighbors, or some high-cost daycare? And what if you want to return to school? These are questions that need to be answered. Not easy as you thought. Oh, one thing I forgot. Where will you live? A shelter, an apartment, with your baby daddy, or with some kindhearted relative?

Decisions, decisions, decisions. If you choose a shelter, it's a temporary life until something better comes along. Any roof over your head is better then living on the streets. Some will even feed you and guide you (hopefully) on adjusting to the outside world. Living with your baby's father, well, that can be a tricky business. Things can got well or blow up in your face. Just know that you have two babies to take care of (your baby and the daddy), and you have to decide which one will need your time more.

If these two are not an option, you can move into your own apartment. Oh yes, your own place. No one in your business, telling you what to do, and how to do things. Paying for your own place, how sweet. But on the other side of the coin, you might want to move in with relatives. That can be good in two ways. One, you can save some money to buy your own place, and two; they can help out some when needed. Just don't crowd each other's space.

The next thing to do is to find work. Bills have to be paid and items for the baby have to be brought. Ask yourself, what work skills do you have? Are you good at anything? If you have to do retail, find a job where you can receive a discount on clothes and household items. The discount may be little, but does go a long way. If movies, music, video games, and books are your hobby, well it's not a good idea to work at these places. Sometimes your hobby needs will come before your child's needs. And without balance, your money will soon slip away. Now are you going to work nights, afternoons, days, weekends, and how many hours a week? How much money do you want to make or how much do you need to live off of? Just know that twenty to twenty-five hours a week is enough to put a little money in your pocket, but it won't pay the bills. Now thirty to forty hours means less time with your child, but more money in your pocket, so you have to ask yourself what is important, money or your child? Remember, all this goes back to the type of skills you have. The more skills you have, the more money you will be able to receive.

That brings us to childcare. Who's going to watch the little bundle of joy while you're out there building a new life? Now with friends and neighbors, you have to be careful. Do you know what goes on in their homes, the company they keep, or if they ever had a prison record for sex crimes or any crime? Remember, you're putting you baby's tiny life in their hands. Now when it comes to family you're a little safer, because you know them and they will be more likely to help. Yes, they are family, but the unanswered question that should be resting in the back of your mind, can you trust them? But whatever you do, please don't take advantage of their helping hand. What are their time limits and how much will it cost you? *Nothing is free.* Remember, you're willing to pay your friends and neighbors, so this means you have to pay your family, too. Now it may not be money, it could be a favor for a favor. If they are charging too much, you're welcome to try daycare. Some people call them the holding pens, where your child sits and wait to you come for them. Daycare is useful; it's just hard to find the right one that will fit your needs. Some are open weekends, six in the morning to six at night, and some are open twenty-four hours. Whatever you do make sure the price is right, and your child is learning valuable things they need to help them along in the future. Make sure they feed your child, and if you have by chance have one of those hard-to-please eaters, see if can you bring that child a lunch, for the simple reason if they don't like it, they won't eat it.

If you have that job and daycare is taken care of, and you're starting to think about going to school to better yourself. While on that road of self-improvement, you will hit many potholes in the road. Your boss may not be willing to work around your schedule. In their mind the job is more important than what you want. No matter how much they say, "We encourage our employees to go back to school," or "Of course we'll work around your schedule," watch your back and don't believe what they have to say. Some bosses will work with or against you. It doesn't have to be school; it could be an appointment for our child. Watch it, there are potholes everywhere, filled with traps to hold you back. You can't avoid them, all you can do is climb over them and keep going. You might have to let that job go and find another one. But know this—keep going, the outside world does get better in time.

It's a cruel world out there for the single mother, with people who won't bend, standing in your way trying to hold you back. Working two or three jobs to make ends meet when the child support payment isn't enough or none at all. We must do things to survive, from legal and illegal jobs, to under the table jobs, and sometimes a job in the sex market (dirty talking on the phone or selling our bodies). Know this and embrace the outside world with open arms.

Most people see a single mother as a charity case or a pet project that needs to be saved. They feel the urge to take us under their wings and perform some good deed to help clear their troubled conscience. Who said that we have a "fix me" sign tattooed on our foreheads? Society, our peers, or maybe ourselves?

Women out there will use friendship as a means to spy. Interweaving in and out of your life, watching and studying how you raise your child, just to find fault in everything you do, while at the same time cheering you on and being your shoulder to cry on. If you're not careful, they will turn your child against you or have you believing you failed as a mother.

Most men think it's their job to fix a single mother. How can they fix us? The only way they know how—sex. That's their answer to all single mothers' problems. Good men who can lay the pipe like no other can. We should be so happy that they are willing to fix us from the bedroom on out. Because we have that brand on our head that says, "I am looking for a do me right man or a handyman." They will do odd fix-it jobs around the house to make it seem their presence is very important to your well-being, while the whole time playing daddy to your child. Before you know it, his toothbrush and personal items are resting in the bathroom, underwear in the drawer, his favorite beer in the refrigerator, and there's an extra plate for dinner every night. His laundry is mixing with yours and you're asking yourself, when he moved in, all he did was hung a few pictures?

The ones who are walking around with their fix-me shades on need to open their eyes to what's really going on around them. A child of a single mother may not have the latest gym shoes and gadgets, fancy hairdos, and their closets may not be filled with designer clothes. Before you jump to conclusion in your mind of illusion, please know our children aren't missing out on anything. It's not what they wear, but who they are. We're fixing them on the inside, to balance off the strike against them for growing up in a single family home. Their inner peace is more important than the newest outerwear and the latest gadgets.

For the men who believe they are seeing a label when it's no label to be actually found, this is for you. If we are looking for a handyman, the best place to find one is in the nearest yellow pages. My fingers can do the walking. Now when it come to a do right man, there's only one person to full that order. It's the Lord, and we pray to him every chance we get. He's our handyman and do right man all rolled up in one.

Before you jump to the charity, fix-them-up bandwagon, you need to know this, your typical single mother doesn't walk around with her hands out, begging on her knees for help. Now don't get us wrong, if you're offering, we'll gladly accept it. But don't think or believe there will be strings attached, so you can hold it over our heads every chance you get. We owe you nothing and asked for nothing in return. You should know this, when something breaks, it has to be fixed. But how can you fix what was never broken in the first place?

Broken Seal

Regrets: remorse, implying a sense of sorrow about events in the past, usually wrongs committed or errors made.

Hush little baby
Don't say a word
Mama's going to
Buy you a mockingbird.
If that mockingbird
Don't sing,
Mama's going to
Buy you a diamond ring.
If that diamond ring
Don't shine,
Mama's going to buy
You a billy goat.
If that billy goat
Gets bony,

> Mama's going to
> Buy you a spotted pony.
> If that pony runs away ...

Words to a lullaby, unfulfilled promises we make to a child. There will be regrets, disappointments, and many nights of shed tears. In the back of our minds, in that little space behind closed doors. If you sit there and say you don't have any, then you're lying to yourself.

Everyone carries around bundles of regrets and disappointments, some more than others. But for a single mother, her burdens are great, always a reminder of how things should of, could of, would of have been. The sweet sounds of that lullaby constantly play in our heads, haunting our dreams, reminding us over and over again where we went wrong. Hush little baby don't say a word, mama's going to buy ... now can we buy when there's no money to buy with?

Every now and then we reach in the back of our minds, and crack open our burdens of regrets and disappointments. To see if they have changed, or disappeared, or have been accomplished, but mostly to see if they are still real. These words of regrets will rush through our minds, creeping back into our thoughts, filling us with self-doubt and reminding us of what we want to forget. Tears of shame and remembrance fill our pillow. When the numbness finally wears off, you tell yourself how can you forget, when the burdens are always there constantly reminding you of all the little and big things you have done wrong? No one will see them or understand, but there they are chasing us and stalking us, our poor misfortunes.

- Was my timing right to have a child?
- Am I being punished for having a child out of wedlock?
- Should I have waited to get married?
- Would things be different if I finished high school or college?
- Is it my fault that my child's father doesn't come around?
- Should I have stayed at that belittling job as a means to provide for my child?
- I am only stripping and selling drugs as a means to provide for my child?
- Why can't I plan a family vacation like everyone else?
- Who is the baby's father?
- How will I pay for the child's education?
- I'm embarrassed or ashamed of living in a car, a shelter, or even the streets.
- I feel that I'm a burden to my family.
- Shame that I had to move in with friends or relatives.
- Worry that I am a failure as a mother.
- Will I turn my child against me by not showing enough love?
- I'm upset with myself because I'm not strong enough.
- If I kill myself or leave that child, would they be better off without me?
- If I have a life and try to reach my dreams, will my child be neglected?
- Should I get married so my child will have a real father?
- If I meet someone and start dating, am I neglecting my child for doing this?

For a single mother, regrets and disappointments will always be there knocking. How we handle them is the question. Some drink, eat, and smoke, work two or three jobs, use drugs and sex to forget the pain, simply bury it, or push ourselves even harder. We relock the seal to our burdens, placing it back behind the closed door in our mind. Once again we numb ourselves to the world around us.

Hush little baby
Don't say a word
Mama's going to
Buy you a MP3 player.
If that MP3 player
Gets broke,
Mama's going to
Buy you a video game.
Nothing to play your
Video game on,
Mama's going to
Buy you a flat screen TV.
Bored with that,
Mama's going to
Buy you a pit bull.
If that pit bull bites someone,
Mama's going to buy you an
Old school car.
If that car runs out of gas,
Mama's going to try a
Little harder to
Prove her love.

Was it Worth It?

Lo, children are an heritage of the Lord:
And the fruit of the womb is his rewards.
Psalms 127-v3

As your little one sleeps so peacefully in bed, a single mother can't help but wonder if everything we went through, and are going through, is worth it. Secretly smiling to yourself, we know the answer to that question in our heart of hearts. Yeah, it's worth it. From every diaper change, spit up, to every bump and bruise, you can't help but thank the Lord for your little blessing. Sometimes you wonder how life would be and what path you would have taken, if you didn't have this child. For now, this little one brings balance to your life.

You found your inner strength by breaking out of that protective shield that's easily placed around you. When you and everyone thought that it was impossible, this child will find a way to crack, break, and weed their way into your life and richen it by teaching you love, joy, peace, patience, kindness, goodness, gentleness, and self-control. Never thought a baby can teach you anything? It's funny how amazing they are in their own special way.

Love is patient and kind; does not envy or boast; is not
arrogant or rude. It does not insist on its own way; it is not
irritable or resentful; it does not rejoice at wrongdoing, but
rejoices with the truth. Love bears all things, believes all things,
hopes all things, endures all things. Love never ends.
1 Corinthians 13 v4-8

Sometimes you will feel that it's not worth it, not getting the help you need, dealing with your baby's father and maybe their family. That one phone call every three to four months, showing up on birthdays and major holidays is not enough. You have to look into their little eyes and see the sadness on their faces as they watch other children playing with their fathers. You have to try your best to explain, without damaging the child emotionally, that the other side of the family has little interest in them. Make sure you let them know it's not their fault how things turn out.

As it was stated before, it's worth it. But it's a lifestyle most single mothers wouldn't choose to do again. For the simple reason of the heartache, stress, money, and sacrifices that have to be made. Sometimes you have to put your life needs and wants on hold for this child. You will lose, find, and recreate yourself on this path to find your inner strength. But know this, and live by this saying for the happiness of you and your child:

"We may not have much, but
together we have it all."

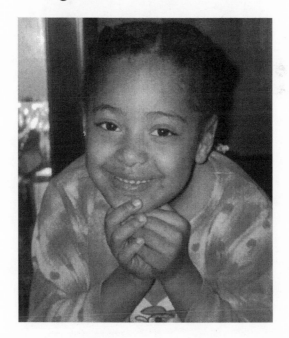

Support Groups for Single Mothers

Check your state's Web site for additional support

Alabama Support

<u>Family Guidance Center of Alabama</u>
Counseling, support groups, parenting classes, and mentoring for families and children in Montgomery, Birmingham, Troy, and Dothan.

2358 Fairlane Drive,
Montgomery, AL 36116
(800) 499-6597
www.familyguidancecenter.org

<u>Family Services Center of Huntsville and Madison County</u>
Non-profit counseling agency for families, children, and other individuals.

P.O. Box 368
Huntsville, AL 35804
(256) 880-1967
www.csna.org

Connecticut Support

<u>Child and Family Agency of Southeastern Connecticut</u>

Provides programs dealing with child abuse, family violence, teen pregnancy, children's health care, childcare, parenting, child guidance, and family preservation.

(860) 767-0147 *Middlesex*
(860) 437-4550 *New London*
www.cfapress.org

<u>The Children's Law Center of CT</u>

Provides indigent children with experienced lawyers who give them a voice in family court. Also provides information in legal matters involving children and advocates in support of legislative policies that advance the well-being and best interests of children.

30 Arbor Street
Hartford, CT 06106
(860) 232-9993
www.clcct.org

Georgia Support

<u>Center for Black Women's Wellness</u>

Wellness programs, teen pregnancy prevention programs and information, and referral services.

477 Windsor St., Suite 309
Atlanta, GA 30312
(404) 688-9202

<u>CHRIS Homes</u>

Family-centered, multi-service agency that provides mental health treatment services to children and families in metro Atlanta. Operates nine therapeutic group homes, two independent living programs, and a variety of community programs that help children and families in crisis.

3111 Clairmont Rd., Suite B
Atlanta, GA 30329
(404) 486-9034

<u>Families First</u>

Services include individual and family counseling, teen pregnancy programs, and educational programs. Located in Atlanta.

P.O. Box 7948
Atlanta, GA 30357
(404) 853-2800

Idaho Support

<u>Treasure Valley Community Resources</u>

Directory of community resources, information, and referrals.

2412 E. Chicago St. #110
Caldwell, ID 83605
(208) 459-9263

<u>Families Anonymous</u>

(800) 736-9805

Illinois Support

<u>Camp Algonquin</u>

Residential camp sessions for youth, mothers, children, and senior adults experiencing financial hardship

**1889 Cary Rd
Algonquin, IL 60102
(847) 658-8212**

Indiana Support

<u>Faith Biblical Counseling Ministries</u>

Free marriage, family, and individual counseling. Located in Lafayette.

Faith Ministries
5526 St. Rd. 26 E.
Lafayette IN 47905
(765) 448-1555

<u>Family Services, Inc. of Lafayette</u>

Services include marriage, family, and individual counseling, parenting
classes, and family programs.

Family Services, Inc.
731 Main Street
Lafayette, IN 47901
(800) 875-5361
(765) 423-5361

Iowa Support

Foundation 2

24-hour crisis hotline, youth shelter, individual and family counseling, and outreach and after-school programs for vulnerable youth. Located in Cedar Rapids.

1714 Johnson Avenue N.W.
Cedar Rapids, IA 52405
319-362-2174 *24-Hour*

Youth and Shelter Services

Provides community youth development, prevention, education, treatment, and residential services to children, youth, and families. Located in Ames.

P.O. Box 1628
Ames, IA 50010
(515) 233-2330
(800) 600-2330 *24 Hour*
Families Anonymous
(800) 736-9805
(913) 342-1110

Maine Support

<u>The Teen and Young Parent Program of Knox County</u>

University of Maine program provides free parenting education to teen and young adult parents, home visitation and mentoring, assistance with locating community support resources, and social events for young parents and their children.

PO Box 805
231 B Park Street
Rockland, ME 04841
(207) 594-1980

Maryland Support

<u>Baptist Family and Children's Services of Maryland and Delaware</u>

Information and referral, mentoring, parenting programs, short-term placements.

**7175 Columbia Gateway Dr, Suite F
Columbia, MD 21046
(800) 621-8834**

<u>Florence Crittenton of Greater Washington</u>

Services and programs for adolescent girls, low income pregnant women and teen mothers in the Washington, D.C. metropolitan area.

**815 Silver Spring Avenue
Silver Spring, MD 20910
(301) 565-9333**

Michigan Support

<u>Father Patrick Jackson Program for Pregnant Teens and Teen Moms</u>

Serves homeless, pregnant, and parenting teens and their children through information and referral regarding adolescent pregnancy, as well as residential and community-based supportive services.

1212 Griswold
Detroit, MI 48226
(734) 761-1440

<u>Covenant House Michigan</u>

Provides shelter and services to children and youth who are homeless, runaways, or at great risk.

2959 Martin Luther King Jr Blvd
Detroit, MI 48208
(313) 463-2000
(800) 999-9999 *24 Hour*

<u>Single Mothers of Color</u>
Advocacy organization for working single mothers of color that develops families.<u>www.smocdenver.org</u>

<u>Catholic Social Services of Grand Rapids</u>

Parent and family support services, behavioral and family counseling, teen parent program, and child welfare services.

40 Jefferson Ave SE
Grand Rapids, MI 49503
(616) 456-1443

Minnesota Support

<u>The Bridge for Runaway Youth</u>

Emergency shelter for youth (ages 10-17), transitional living program for homeless youth (ages 16-20), family-centered counseling, 24-hour walk-in counseling for youth and parents (no appointment necessary).

2200 Emerson Ave.
Minneapolis, MN 55407
(612) 377-8800 *24 Hour*

<u>Chrysalis, A Center for Women</u>

Mental health clinic in Minneapolis providing legal assistance, education and family support.

4432 Chicago Avenue South
Minneapolis, MN 55407
(612) 871-0118

<u>Family Attachment and Counseling Center of Minnesota</u>

Specializes in working with attachment disorder and serving the needs of adoptive and foster families.

18322C Minnetonka Blvd.
Deephaven, MN 55391
(952) 475-2818

<u>Lutheran Social Services of Minnesota</u>

Largest statewide non-profit social service agency in Minnesota with services and programs for children, youth, and families.

2485 Como Avenue
St. Paul, MN 55108
(800) 582-5260

<u>Resource Center for Fathers and Families</u>

Six offices in the Minneapolis/St. Paul metropolitan area offer parenting classes, support groups, anger management classes, family law seminars, and relationship workshops.

Human Services Building, Suite 305
1201 89th Avenue NE
Blaine, Minnesota 55434
(763) 783-4938

Mississippi Support

<u>Family Crisis Services of Northwest Mississippi</u>

Family support services to Oxford and Lafayette Counties and the University of Mississippi community. Includes counseling, workshops, teen pregnancy prevention, mentoring, and 24-hour crisis intervention.

(662) 234-9929
(800) 230-9929

Missouri Support

<u>Missouri Volunteer Resource Mothers</u>

Mentoring program for pregnant and parenting teens.

303 Gentry Hall
Columbia, MO 65211
(573) 884-0644

Nebraska Support

<u>Lutheran Family Services of Nebraska</u>

Programs throughout Nebraska include parent support, individual and family counseling, and substance abuse treatment.

120 South 24th Street, Suite 100
Omaha, NE 68102
(402) 342-7007

<u>Northeast Family Center</u>

Neighborhood-based center with a focus on programs to support children, youth, and families.

6220 Logan Ave
Lincoln, NE 68507
(402) 471-3700

Nevada Support

<u>Clark County Family Law Self-Help Center</u>

Legal information and resources to self-represented individuals in divorce, annulment, child custody, visitation rights, and child support.

601 North Pecos Road
Las Vegas, Nevada 89101
(702) 455-1500

<u>Family Support Council of Douglas County</u>

Free services include parenting classes, domestic violence and sexual assault prevention and intervention, mediation, and conflict resolution.

(775) 782-8692

New Hampshire Support

<u>Child and Family Services of New Hampshire</u>

Provides an array of social services to strengthen family life and promote community commitment to the needs of children throughout New Hampshire.

99 Hanover St.
Manchester, NH 03105
(800) 640-6486

New Jersey Support

Family Service of Morris County

Counseling, education, support groups, and other services for children
and families.

62 Elm Street
Morristown, NJ 07960
(973) 538-5260

New Mexico Support

Catholic Charities of Central New Mexico

Family education and counseling services.

**1410 Coal Avenue SW
Albuquerque, NM 87104
(505) 247-9521**

**2010 Bridge SW
Albuquerque, NM 87105
(505) 247-0442**

New York Support

Inwood House

Programs for pregnant teens and teen parents, as well as intervention and prevention programs in New York City.

320 East 82nd St
New York, NY 10028
(212) 861-4400

North Dakota Support

<u>West Dakota Family & Parent Resource Center</u>

Parenting classes, workshops, seminars, resource materials
(877) 264-1142

Oklahoma Support

<u>Catholic Charities of Oklahoma City</u>

Counseling services to individuals, groups, families and children, and residential programs and services for pregnant and parenting teens.

1501 N. Classen Blvd.
Oklahoma City, OK 73106
405-523-3000
800-375-8514

Oregon Support

<u>Albertina Kerr Centers</u>

Care, treatment, counseling, residential placement and education for children, adults, and families at risk or in crisis due to abuse, developmental disabilities, and/or mental health issues. Located in Portland

424 NE 22nd Avenue
Portland, OR 97232
(503) 239-8101
(503) 255-4205

<u>Grandma's House of Central Oregon</u>
Safe, nurturing, and stable shelter to homeless and/or abused pregnant (whether choosing adoption or parenting), and parenting teen mothers between the ages of twelve to nineteen years old and their babies

PO Box 6372
Bend, Oregon 97708
(541) 383-3515

South Carolina Support

<u>Family Service Center</u>

Multi-service agency whose services include individual and family counseling, adolescent pregnancy prevention, and family life enrichment workshops for Fairfield, Lexington, Newberry, Richland, Sumter, Florence, and York Counties.

**1800 Main Street
Columbia, SC 29202
(800) 922-5651
(803) 733-5450**

Texas Support

Christian Homes

Full maternity care and adoption counseling to women experiencing an unplanned pregnancy. Offers adoption services, operates a free maternity home, and works with girls throughout Texas and Oklahoma who do not wish to relocate to Abilene, but want the services of a Christian adoption agency.

1202 Estates Drive
Abilene, Texas 79602
(325) 677-2205
(800)592-4725 *24 Hour*

Vermont Support

<u>The Lund Family Center</u>

Services include therapeutic residential program for pregnant and parenting teens and young women, teen pregnancy prevention program, parent education and support

7 Kilburn Road
Burlington, VT 05401
(802) 864-7467
(800) 639-1741

Virginia Support

<u>Northern Virginia Family Service</u>

Non-profit organization providing services for families in need in the Northern Virginia area.

10455 White Granite Drive
Suite 100
Oakton, VA 22124
(703) 385-3267

Wisconsin Support

<u>Family Resource Center for Eau Claire County</u>

Programs and services that build on family strengths through prevention, education, support, and networking with other resources in the community.

(715) 833-1735

<u>Family Resource Center of Sheboygan County</u>

Information, support, and coordination of resources for families and children.

1209A Eastern Avenue
Plymouth, WI 53073
(920) 892-6706

Turn the page for a sneak preview of D.C. Spencer's next book, a collection of short stories full of betrayal, jealousy, resentment, heartache, and doubt.

Sister's Love

Jacinta was relaxing on the tan couch in the living room, enjoying a day off from work. She was scanning the television for something worthwhile to watch when the afternoon newscaster announced the winner of the Detroit's Businessman of the Year Award. It was her brother-in-law, Chaz. She glared into the television as her sister, Tabitha, stood there playing the loving wife by Chaz' side while he accepted his award. The whole scene turned Jacinta's stomach into knots. She wished that she could go through the television and give her sister the beat-down she so deserved.

She turned off the television. No sense wishing for something she couldn't do. She gazed out of the window, unaware of the beautiful sunny day outside, reminiscing back to the day when she first saw Chaz Washington and Tabitha stole him right from under her nose. All Jacinta knew is that her life and dreams were demolished one night at the Shadow Bar.

It all started three years ago, that one night at her little hangout in Hamtramck, the Shadow Bar, during one of their summer mid-week, after-work affairs. The kind where the ladies get in free before nine and you can have all the hot wings you can eat for twenty-five cents a wing. Jacinta was leaning over one of the upstairs balcony rails, tapping her foot to the beat of some new song by Floetry and skimming the crowded, smoke-filled room for any good prospects when her eyes fell on him. This was the fourth time she had seen him in here this month. Standing against the wall, tall, strong, and handsome with that almond-toasted skin that had just been kissed by the sun. He was wearing a dark suit that was obviously made for his frame. You could see he wasn't one of those men who believe shopping off the rack to buy a ready-to-wear suit. He was always alone, never with a female on his arm; just hanging out, talking to the fellows he came in with and maybe grabbing a couple of females for a dance before heading out.

At that moment Jacinta knew that was the man of her dreams, the one she waited her whole life for, her future husband-to-be. Mustering up the courage to go over to say hello and ask him for a dance, she spotted Tabitha slithering her away across the room to stand all cozy by his side. Charming him with her poison, the same way she did mom and dad. She doesn't even attend places like these; she always said they were beneath her style. But there she was by his side, inching her way up his body to place a kiss on his toasty cheek. He took Tabitha by the hand and led her to the dance floor for a slow dance.

The doorbell rang, pulling Jacinta out of her thoughts and bringing her back to the reality around her. Leaving her comfy spot on the couch, she opened the door.

"Oh, it's you," said Jacinta, dryly turning her nose up at Tabitha.

"I'm glad to see you, too," said Tabitha happily. She's one of those people that no matter how bad things get, they always find something to smile about.

Here they stand mirror images of each other. Two perfectly shaped beauties made from the same mold. Identical from the top of their heads down to their toes, with the same brown complexion, hazel eyes, sandy-brown shoulder length hair, with a little mole on the upper right corner of their mouth. No one can tell them apart, not even their parents.

"So, Jacinta, can I come in?" asked Tabitha.

"Sure." Jacinta stepped aside, wondering what her sister was planning to throw in her face now.

Tabitha came right in and took a seat on the couch, leaving Jacinta with no choice but to sit next to her or take the chair across from her. Deciding on the chair, Jacinta plopped herself down, when she really wanted to go across the room and push Tabitha out of her seat. Tabitha took a quick glance around the room and saw that Jacinta had the same pieces of furniture that their parents gave her two years ago, when she brought them a new set.

"So, Tabitha, what brings you to my side of town? Slumming?"

"Can I just come and visit my favorite big sister?"

"No." The way Tabitha and their parents acted, you would think she was the oldest, when actually Jacinta was born twenty minutes before her.

She looked Jacinta directly in the face. "Well the only reason…."

"Spit it out, will you?" snapped Jacinta.

Tabitha took a deep breath before starting. She was not going to let her sister's impatience rush her. "Well, you know

Mom and Dad's wedding anniversary is coming up in two weeks and I ...."

"I know. What about it?"

"Will you let me finish?" Jacinta let out a loud sigh, while rolling her eyes at Tabitha. "Anyway, I thought it would be nice to send them on an Alaskan cruise, since they always talked about going. And Mom and Dad always said they never had a honeymoon."

"What are you trying to say, Tabitha, that I'm not smart enough to pick out a gift as well as you?" Trying to put some space between them, Jacinta got up and walked towards the kitchen with Tabitha right on her heels.

"Of course not. Do you have some idea of what you plan on given them?" Looking around the kitchen, she noticed the empty can of Vienna sausage and a package of Ramen noodles in the trash, and the open box of crackers on the counter. *Money must be tight this month*, she thought.

"If you must know, I am planning on give them an oil painting of their wedding day," proclaimed Jacinta. "It's already paid for; I just have to pick up next Friday."

"Oh, that's lovely," Tabitha sarcastically remarked, aware of that something that extreme was really out of Jacinta's budget.

"Damn." Tabitha was trying to outshine her again. Just like she did when they were kids. Who had the prettiest dress, which one had the better grades, who could get their parents' love, even who decided on what type of party they would have for their birthday.

"What?"

Tabitha stood there, dumbfounded. She couldn't understand what she did wrong.

"There you go, putting down my ideas again. The same way you do when we were kids. They are my parents, too!" said Jacinta, angrily.

"My goodness, I am just trying to be helpful." Tabitha opened the refrigerator, noticing the items resting on the half-empty, sticky shelves, from three eggs, two containers holding less than a swallow of milk and orange juice, a half-empty jar of peanut and grape jelly spread, and something in a molded plastic package in the corner next to the box of baking soda.

"Jacinta, I know your bank teller job doesn't pay that much and that type of gift is beyond your means."

Jacinta nearly missed Tabitha's face when she slammed the refrigerator door. She couldn't believe that Tabitha would have the gall to come in her house and put her down, always thinking that she's better than someone. One thing for sure, they were not kids anymore, with Mom and Dad breaking up their fights or disagreements, or whatever you want to call it. No this time, today is a new day, Jacinta knows she's not going to stand here taking Tabitha's uppity crap this time. This disrespecting her is going to stop now one way or another, because today the truth is going to set Tabitha free, even if it means breaking her foot off in her ass.

"We maybe be sisters and we may look alike," Jacinta said, trying to calm her anger down so her thoughts could come out clearly. "Oh, you just don't know how much I hate that. Every time I look at you I see my own refection." She pointed her finger in Tabitha's chest. "Every time Mom and Dad look at me, they see me as the twin who's the failure. Poor Jacinta can't get her life together. Why can't she be like her sister, Tabitha? I am sick and tired of you trying to outshine me in front of them."

"I do no such thing. I just know how to make good choices in life. Come on, Jacinta, they love you just as much as they love me."

"I am glad I did what I did," Jacinta said coldly.

"Whatever are you talking about?" Knowing anything was possible when Jacinta got mad, the fear of uncertainty rang out in Tabitha's voice. She remembered the time Jacinta broke the heads off of her dolls and then buried them in the backyard. She made Jacinta take the blame for breaking Mom favorite vase. Jacinta received a butt whipping, punishment for a week, and she couldn't go to Boblo with the church. And the time Jacinta gave the tie she bought for Father's Day to Mack, who lived down the street from them, so he could hang a dead cat from it. All because she told dad, Jacinta cursed him out behind his back, and Jacinta got her butt whipped for that.

"Remember the time I moved back in town, you let me crash at your apartment for about six months?" Tabitha stood there in front of Jacinta. She shook her head in agreement. "Well, I read your journal. You know, your forbidden book, which holds your deepest, darkness secrets."

"You didn't!" Tabitha horrified by what her sister might have read.

"You would write about all the times Chaz wanted to sleep with you, him telling you how his body is aching to be with you. How he would get your panties so drenched that you would need a panty liner." The whole time Jacinta stood there with a grin on her face, laughing to herself, as if she's the only one who knows the punch line.

"Oh, before I forget, remember the time Chaz went out of town for a week and left you something to think of him while he's gone?" Jacinta rubbed her breast with her hand. "A passion mark on your left breast?"

Tabitha realized her sister been spying on her. "I can't believe I let you stay in my home."

"Whatever, Tabitha, you did. Remember the time you thought you and Chaz had the place to yourselves for some alone time? For the record, I saw *everything*."

"You heifer!" exploded Tabitha, as she loss her rich-girl composure that she worked so hard to keep and maintain.

"I cracked the door; there you were both naked in bed. I would have to say that Chaz has one hell of a sexy body, which I knew he would. You teased, led him on. You …"

"I wasn't ready and I wanted to wait till I got married," blurted Tabitha, fighting back the tears.

"You stole him from me!" yelled Jacinta. "Chaz was going to be my man. I saw him first and you took him!"

"I didn't." Tabitha didn't have the foggiest idea what Jacinta talking about. "We were dating off and on for about a year or two before we decided to get married."

"Like always, if I want it, you take it." Getting up in her sister's face. "Tabitha, you can't handle a man like Chaz."

As she questioned Jacinta, Tabitha, took a firm grip of her arm, wondering what other bombshell she's going to drop on her. "What did you do?'

"I did what any real woman would have done, I gave Chaz what he wanted and needed. You know a good bone." As those words left Jacinta's mouth, Tabitha answered them with a hard slap to Jacinta's face.

She wiped away the blood from her lip. "I guess you feel that I deserve that. The man is a excellent lover," Jacinta said, standing there with a smug look on her face. "Was he upset to find out that you were still a virgin on your wedding night?"

"You, you …"

"Everything you have should be mine!"

Made in the USA
Lexington, KY
22 November 2009